Over the Creek

Heartfelt Poetry ———

Valery Frazier Kelley

authorHOUSE®

AuthorHouse™
1663 Liberty Drive
Bloomington, IN 47403
www.authorhouse.com
Phone: 833-262-8899

© 2020 Valery Frazier Kelley. All rights reserved.

No part of this book may be reproduced, stored in a retrieval system, or transmitted by any means without the written permission of the author.

Published by AuthorHouse 05/31/2022

ISBN: 978-1-6655-2512-1 (sc)
ISBN: 978-1-6655-2511-4 (e)

Library of Congress Control Number: 2021909394

Print information available on the last page.

Any people depicted in stock imagery provided by Getty Images are models, and such images are being used for illustrative purposes only. Certain stock imagery © Getty Images.

This book is printed on acid-free paper.

Because of the dynamic nature of the Internet, any web addresses or links contained in this book may have changed since publication and may no longer be valid. The views expressed in this work are solely those of the author and do not necessarily reflect the views of the publisher, and the publisher hereby disclaims any responsibility for them.

Acknowledgment

I am grateful for my Aunts and Uncles who remain amongst us and those who have gone on to glory. I must name those who helped to mold and shape my life—the Carter's and Frazier's. The Carter's are Leander, Jr. (Barbara), Gorham (Doll), Charles (Cat), Shirley (Gene), Edward (Jean), Pat (Mildred), Quentin (Noreen), Hattie (Pete), Dora, Selinda (Ross), Lillian (Jewett), Mary and Raymond (Mary).

Special thanks to my mentor, Jennettia Carter Drake, who has encouraged and supported me through the years as well!

May this book encourage and inspire you to follow your dreams and accomplish your goals.

Contents

Acknowledgment v

Family And Friends

My Husband.. 3
To My Daughter, Ja'Va 4
Daddy's Girl 5
Christopher.. 6
My Siblings... 7
Sister, Keep the faith 8
Ma Pauline 9
Friendship 11
Family... 12
Friendship 14
Friends are for 15
Don't Think I think I Am Above 17
Ayden Christopher 19
Overcoming 21
God's Healing Power 23
No Ill.. 24
Breathe On Me 25
You're The Greatest 27
We'll Miss You 28
I'll Be Rejoicing... 29
He's On Time.. 31
Focusing 32
Sweet Caroline 33
Family of Faith.. 35

Young At Heart.. 37

Mother

Dedicated to my Mother "Anna Bell Carter Frazier" 41
A Giving Mother 44
A Mother's Love.. 46

Birthday

A Grand Celebration... 49
Friendship 51
True Frienship... 52
This Day.. 54
Happy Birthday 56
Happy Wedding Anniversary 58
Happy Birthday, Linda.. 60
Happy Birthday 62
My Relative 63
Celebration 65
Celebration 67

Love

Unlimited Love.. 72
Maybe I Am 73
While I'm Yours And You Are Mine................................. 75
I Desire A Partner 77
Not One 78
My Candy.. 80
Real Close 81
I Care So Much... 83

Let	85
My Life	87
Class Reunion	90
I Knew It Had To Be You	92
To Have And To Hold	93
You Are Complete	94
My Baby Brother, Freddie	95
Life For Me	96
We Were There	98
Our Neighbors, Our Friend	99
Cousin Joe	101
Safe In His Arms	102

Retirement / Work

Happy Retirement	107
Retirement Celebration	109
Happy Retirement	111
Safe in His Arms	113
Farewell	115
At FSC	117
Happy Retirement	118
Doing Your Thing	119
Retirement Celebration	121
On Your Retirement	123
My Retirement	125

Religious

The Woman's Plight	129
God Knew	131
God is Good	133

I Wonder, Yet I know 134
Peace On Earth 135
This Time 136
Much Appreciative 137
Touch Not 139

Social

The Wants of Freedom 143
Give Me Credit 145
Parts of Me 146

Death

See Ya Later...... Uncle Buddy 149
My Grandma 150
You're Alright Now 151
Missing Grandma 154
Upon Death 156

My Husband

To: James C. Kelley

It's good to know you have support
And someone's by your side...
And that when a need is solved
It's done so with such pride...
It's good to know you have a shoulder
To laugh or cry upon...
And that business will continue
When your life on earth is done...
It's good to know you have a savior
And the one you love serves God too...
And that prayer is always in order
You've offered it our whole relationship through...
It's good to know that I can count on you
To answer when I call...
I'm grateful for all you do and have done
The big things and the small...

To My Daughter, Ja'Va

With love: Mommy

Since our hearts first met
Life hasn't been the same . . .
The waking up at early morning
The deciding upon your name . . .

I long to see your smile
And love to hear your voice . . .
Having you is such a joy
Not just a matter of choice . . .

I love your little hands
I'm amazingly watching them grow . . .
And all other parts of your body
From your head down to your toes . . .

Your eyes are so beautiful
Your hair's so softly curled . . .
I embrace you into my life
I welcome you into this world . . .

Daddy's Girl

To: Ja'Va Paris Kelley
Concerning: Your father, James

When daddy holds you in his arms
He whispers, "I love this little girl"
No one out there could take your place
In this old sinful world . . .

He can't stand to hear you cry
He'll look at me and say . . .
Valery, what's wrong with her
And I'll reply, "She'll be okay" . . . .

He's so thankful to God
And he acknowledges it when he pray . . .
In the morning, noon or night
The beginning and ending our day. . .

He prays to God for protection
To keep your body healthy and strong. . .
And that you'll learn to ask for forgiveness
As your lifetime journeys on. . .

Christopher
1/16/02

You're my little man
I think the world of you. . .
Having a son is such fulfillment
And just watching the things you do. . .

You offer me so much love
You hold me, Oh so tight. . .
For you are my company keeper
In the sleepless, dark of nights. . .

You're my great supporter
I can just already tell. . .
That you'll be in my corner
When things aren't going well. . .

You already make me proud
And I long to see you grow. . .
Always remember that Mommy loves you
Ask me things you'd like to know. . .

My Siblings

To: Barry, Dee, Shirley, Deline & Ricky

Barry is the fastest one

Oh my could he run..

He loved to hang out with buddies

And have a lot of fun...

Dee is the shop-a-holic

Loves pocketbooks and shoes...

She will spend her last dime

Giving to others that she choose...

Shirley is the lover of books

She really loves to read...

She'll stay up all night to complete one

And loves doing special deeds...

Deline is the family clown

He tells lifetime stories that are true...

He'll have you laughing on your knees

And crying when he's through...

Ricky is the youngest of us

He's considerate, humble and kind...

His conversations are encouraging

Let him share what's on his mind...

---------------------------- ----------------------------

Sister, Keep the faith

To: Deborah Frazier

No matter how difficult things may seem
Keep on trusting in Jesus name
Don't give up this Christian fight
Hang in there with all your might

Although you have not all you need
Money often short, not cause of greed
Still, keep holding to his hands
Only God sometimes understands

Because you often give so much
And has that perfect final touch
Who could deny you when you call
Though short in stature, your heart is tall

Now when my words shall come to end
I know it's you I can depend
To always say, that's just her way
Keep the faith until judgement day

Ma Pauline

"In celebration of your 90th Birthday May 13, 2001"

We are all on one accord
Realizing that "Just one rose will do"...
But, we thank you for your many prayers
And for helping to bring us through...

Through some very trying times
When we were sick, you gave advice...
And when we got in trouble
You told of Jesus' sacrifice...

You've taught us right from wrong
And stood by Daddy Raymond's side...
No matter how difficult times got
You'd walk with him with pride...

You always knew how to save
A dollar, a penny or a dime...
And you still can do the mess around
At any given time...

So, when the "Handwriting is on the wall"
And God has called your name. . .
We'll all be able to identify
The characteristics of "Ma Pauline". . .

We love you,
The Family 5/26/01

Friendship

I need not search for a friend
While there's someone like you...
There isn't need to strain my eyes
In dark skies or in blue...
Why should I stop to wonder
When I know that you'd be there?
If ever I should need your help
I'd come to you, you care...
What can I attach to you
A title that seems unclear...?
But you've gained my respect
Cause you're someone that's dear...
I have had to stop and say
"What's the matter with this man..."
But, really I know why you reacted
As you did, I understand...
Now, such things are behind us
And we both know the deal...
So, try to take life easy
Do only as you feel...

Family

September 1, 2001
Family Reunion

Some of us are doers
We'll do what must be done . . .
Won't wait on anybody else
Then join in the fun . . .

Some of us are complainers
No matter what-something's not right . . .
I think some don't get any sleep
Plan all through the night . . .

Some of us are behind the scenes
We'll lend a helping hand . . .
While other just won't chip in
I don't care who takes the stand . . .

Some of us are listeners
We'll lend a listening ear . . .
We're there to give comfort
When the other needs a cheer . . .

Some of us are lovers
We love everybody – one and all . . .
We don't carry hatred in our hearts
And we'll help right from the start . . .

Some of us are late birds
No matter what's at stake . . .
We just love to take our time
Having other people wait . . .

Some of us are sincere
We constantly give our best . . .
We're going to work til Jesus comes
To give us that final test . . .

Friendship

You're such a kind and thoughtful friend
Who reached out to all . . .
With all the love and warmth you give
Each patient you tempt to spoil . . .

And even when you socialize
You encourage so much fun . . .
You're the leader of any pack
Your work seems never done . . .

I wish only the best for you
As you prepare to leave . . . .
I'm saddened by the very thought
That some of us may grieve . . .

But, I believe deep down
Due to your personality . . .
God will watch over you
And bring another friend to me . . .

Friends are for

Friends are for the sunshine
When all you see is rain
Friends are for laughter
When all you feel is pain
Friends are for uplifting
When you are down and out
Friends are for reassuring
When you are full of doubt
Friends are for smiling
When you want to wear a frown
Friends are for accompanying you
When you desire no one to be around
Friends are for supporting
When you think you're all alone
Friends are for contacting
When you are far away from home
Friends are for disagreeing
When you are headed to the wrong way
Friends are for interjecting
When you are lost of words to say
Friends are for surprising

When you just know all has forgotten
Friends are for cutting around it
When you just know the apple's rotten
Friends are for showing kindness
When you are eager to complain
Friends are for just knowing
When you don't know how to explain . . .
That's what Friends are for!

Don't Think I Think I Am Above

To: Mrs. Sheila Teel
Sunday, May 26, 2013

Don't think I think I am above
God has given me a plan . . .
And I will work hard while it's day
Until I leave this land . . .

Don't think I think I am above
I am in the same boat as some . . .
I was taught to hold my head up high
Until the battle is won . . .

Don't think I think I am above
Because of the clothes I wear . . .
I'd have each of you to know
Life has been no crystal stare . . .

Don't think I think I am above
Because of my elegant style . . .
I walked to church and I walked to school
These feet put on some miles . . .

Don't think I think I' am above
I've given God my heart . . .
So when my mission is complete
You can say I've done my part . . .

------------------------- -------------------------

Ayden Christopher

To: Ms. Karen Wright
4/13/13

May God bless your precious little one
Who's soon coming to this world . . .
May have wondered if it'd be
A precious boy or girl . . .

So, technology says you're carrying
A 6lbs & something little boy . . .
So, Zachariah will be able to share
His special favorite little toy

It's good he'll have a playmate
And Tot will have to share her love . . .
We're happy about your gift "Ayden Christopher"
Given to you from Heaven above . . .

Mrs. Simmons can add another Great-Grand
To children she's helped raise . . .
And Sis Dee can continue babysitting
Our family will gladly be her aide . . .

You were blessed by your nurturing
We're here to lend a helping hand . . .
God knows what's truly best for you
And it's all according to His plan . . .

Overcoming

To: William Shiver

Although I thought I had it all
All I had was lost
Due to my habitual way of living
I failed to detect what it would cost

I knew I had a lovely home
That I worked hard to build
And yet it was a struggle to keep
Because of my desire to yield

I bowed to an illegal temptation
That just drained my every thought
That just drove away my pleasures
The choice of drugs I chose and bought

I've learned to focus on brighter things
That's not damaging to me
Yes it took some time to realize
In drugs is not the way to be

For I've developed community impact
As an outreach to mankind
For those who needs assistance
Due to drug abuse or has it in mind

Now I am determined
To help those of you in need
By educating and counseling folk all over the world
By doing various deeds

I openly confessed of my doings
And now at peace am I
Since I decided that I wanted to live
By God's grace I have not died

God's Healing Power

I whispered a prayer to God for you
That you would be alright . . .
I asked that your pain be taken away
And that you'd rest during the night . . .

And often during my prayers
Needed strength, I asked for too . . .
That I'd understand the mystery
Of what's going on with you . . .

But, through it all
Your condition has made me see . . .
That life is far more precious
Than diamonds, furs, or other luxuries . . .

Perhaps to just be thankful
For things we fail to treasure . . .
And to realize God's healing power
Is far more than one can measure . . .

No Ill

To: Francene Scott

Keep believing in God Almighty
He will heal your body and soul . . .
Just stay on the path of righteousness
And give Him full control . . .

Keep looking towards heaven
And your eyes clear of mote . . .
Stay strong on the battlefield
To his Kingdom say, "I devote" . . .

Keep on the straight and narrow
And your heart full of love divine . . .
Know that He is watching over you
He will step in on time . . .

Keep your body pure and holy
Use it only to do His will . . .
Know your healing is in the making
Trust God who knows no ill . . .

Breathe On Me

Lord, take a moment to lend an ear
To help me cope with "Why" . . .
Do I feel you've allowed some things
To simply make me cry . . .

I'm feeling a bit discouraged
And often times alone . . .
I want my house to be perfected
Yet, my mind reflects of back home . . .

I'm reminded of my Uncle
Who was full of life . . .
And my Husband's Ex
Who has caused us both some strife . . .

I know you will hear my plea
And make by burdens light . . .
I often call you my savior
And call you day and night . . .

Dear Lord, Breathe on me
And keep me from all harm . . .
Protect my inner feelings from
Those deceitful charm . . .

I'm trusting in your judgement
As you lend your ear my way . . .
Thanks for keeping me humble
Be with me throughout my day . . .

You're The Greatest

4/25/12

"Secretaries Day"

It doesn't matter what we need

Or what someone may request. . .

You try hard to take care of it

While doing your very best. . .

It doesn't matter what time we call

To say we're not coming or may be late. . .

You'll simply pass the message on

And is efficient with recording our dates. . .

It doesn't matter which Department

That you're called upon to serve. . .

We call you the greatest of Secretaries

That this Fleet Readiness Center has ever heard. . .

So, allow us to recognize you

Give you your flowers while you live. . .

And thank you for your assistance

And the hard work ethics you instill. . .

------------------------ ------------------------

We'll Miss You

To: Lou Ann Mallady
01/20/00

FOR ALL THE HELP YOU WILLINGLY GIVE
AND ALL THE LOVE YOU SHOW...
WE REALLY HATE THAT YOU'RE LEAVING
YET, WE KNOW YOU MUST GO...
YOU'VE BEEN SUCH AN ASSET
YOU'VE GIVEN YOUR ALL AND ALL
SO, WHEN THE PROMOTION OPPORTUNITY ARRIVED
YOU READILY SAID, "YES" TO THE CALL...
NONE OF US CAN BLAME YOU
FOR WANTING MORE AND DESERVING IT, TOO...
SO, WE WISH THE BEST LIFE OFFERS
MAY YOUR SPIRITS BEGIN ANEW...
GOD BLESS YOU AS YOU BEGIN
A CHALLENGING JOB AHEAD...
YOU MUST KNOW THAT WE'LL MISS YOU
WE'LL CHERISH THE MEMORIES OF TASK YOU'VE LED...

I'll Be Rejoicing

To: Margaret N. Johnson

I DISLIKE WORKING OVER HERE
CONTRACTS IS NOT MY CUP OF TEA
I DID NOT ASK TO COME TO THIS PLACE
ESPECIALLY NOT TO BE THE SECRETARY
I DISLIKE WHEN I'M MISUSED
OR, MY SKILLS NOT BEING EXPOSED
AND NARROW MINDED PERSONNEL
WHO DON'T DO AS THEY SUPPOSE
I DISLIKE THE ASSUMPTION
THAT I SHOULD JUST BE GLAD
THAT I'M NOT OUT THE GATE
OH, THAT REALLY MAKES ME MAD
I DISLIKE WHEN GROWN UPS
HAVE TO BE WATCHED IN FRONT AND BACK
BUT, I MIGHT AS WELL STOP COMPLAINING
AND STRAIGHTEN UP MY ACT
I MIGHT AS WELL GET ON THE BALL
FILL OUT APPLICATIONS LEFT AND RIGHT
EVEN AS IF IT CAUSES ME
TO STAY UP HALF THE NIGHT

I MIGHT AS WELL ENGAGE DAILY
IN SOMETHING THAT WILL MAKE ME SMILE
I'M JUST GRATEFUL THAT I CAN WORK
BEING THAT I'M STUCK HERE FOR A WHILE
I'M REALLY NOT COMPLAINING
I JUST TELL IT AS I SEE
ONE DAY I'LL BE REJOICING
WITH THAT MAN FROM GALILEE

He's On Time

NO MATTER WHAT YOU'RE GOING THROUGH
HOW DARK THE ROAD MAY SEEM. . .
GOD KNOWS HOW TO LIGHTEN YOU
HE BRIGHTENS THE LOWEST BEAM. . .
IN ANY SITUATION WHERE
WE FEEL OUR WORK IS DONE. . .
HE GUIDES US ON TO HIGHER HEIGHTS
WE KNOW OUR VICTORY'S WON. . .

SO, AS YOU JOURNEY THROUGHOUT LIFE
AND WHATEVER PATH YOU TAKE. . .
KNOW YOUR PRESENCE HERE
WAS WITH MEANING
AND NOT A BIG MISTAKE. . .
WE HOPE THAT YOU'LL BE HAPPY
AND THAT YOUR CAREER WILL CLIMB. . .
KEEP YOUR EYE ON THE SPARROW
AND KNOW THAT GOD IS ON TIME. . .

Focusing

ONE MUST SEARCH DEEP WITHIN TO JUSTIFY ACTIONS

TRY TO BE HONEST, UPFRONT WITH HOW THEY FEEL

TRY TO UTILIZE ENERGY WITHIN FOCUS ON SELF

AND HOW LIFE'S HIGHWAY SEEMS UPHILL

ONE MUST DEFINE THE INNER MAN

NOTIFY PARTICIPANTS OF THE OUTCOME

NOT BE AMAZED AT THE RESULTS

BUT BE RECEPTIVE OF THE ROLLED DRUM

ONE MUST REMAIN ELIGIBLE FOR IMPROVEMENT

BE THE RAISED HAND WHEN IN THE KNOW

BE THE QUESTIONED VOICE WHEN IN DOUBT

AND THE RECOGNIZER OF THE PASSIONATE GLOW

ONE MUST REITERATE THE UNNOTICED

DEMONSTRATE THE STABILITY OF THE MIND

ILLUSTRATE BY ANY MEANS AVAILABLE

HOW ONE SHOULD BE DEFINED

Sweet, Caroline

To: Caroline Harkley

You've been right there for the family
Whatever was the need
You took charge when "Ms Minnie" died
You taught us to take heed . .

Whenever we need help
And you can lend a helping hand
Your arms are stretched out wide
You do the best you can . .

You've been right there for the family
You'll say "Lord, that ain't right"
And for many prayerful situations
You're on your knees at night . . .

Not often do we have to wonder
How you feel about this and that
You definitely speak your peace
And let us know where you're at . . .

You raised three beautiful children
Pactically on your own
But you learned at an early age
You're not in this race alone . . .

You love to hear good singing
And you love to catch good sales
We love hear you folklore and listen to your old tales

So we've come to show some love
And appreciation for you this way
Thank God you lived to witness
Family and friends at your gathering today . . . .

Family of Faith

To: The Chatman-Richards Family Reunion
July 2011

There's something about family ties
When you search the family tree
You'll find many names revealed
From slavery to being free

Sometimes our actions are questioned
We wonder why things are said and done
We must reach out with love and sincerity
Guiding the lost to the HOLY ONE

This family truly exercise faith
We know God is always near
We've learned to put our Trust in HIM
Who casts out doubt and fear

Out love for each is very unique
There is a bond that's strong
I'd say our motto is quite the same
"If I can help someone along" ..

Let's keep each other encouraged
Let's try hard to refrain
From envy, strife and jealousy
That destroys a family's name

So, let there be peace among us
Let love and joy abide
Enjoy our Family Reunion
And let there be no divide

Young At Heart

To: Teno Jones

A life well deserving of complete happiness
Is what's desired for you . . .
Although it seems so far from reach
Allow God to see you through . . .

It may not happen just now
Or maybe tomorrow may even seem late . . .
But keep believing and trusting
For God somehow knows which date . . .

Oh, you may have already tried
To give up and just give in . . .
But something or someone told you
You have a greater friend. . .

Oh, you may have reached a point
Where even Mom couldn't understand . . .
But in the midst of trying
She gave to God your hand . . .

Yes, your life can be uncertain
Or so it may seem that way . . .
But, you're part of the controller
When rewinded said, "its okay" . . .

I'd like to commend you
For enduring what you start . . .
Not all possess the ability
To stay young at heart . . .

Mother

Dedicated to my Mother
"Anna Bell Carter Frazier"

We Honor You. . . . .
9-5-93

We know it's not often said
Or much is ever done
To show you that we love you
And consider you number one

We've all come to celebrate
How proud we are of you
For all the hard work you've done
And all you try to do

You're the oldest girl of nine children
So, we know you had it rough
Trying to help your mother with the chores
The road has sometimes been real tough

But, with God there to guide you
And to show you directions to take
We know you'll keep the assurance
Knowing God forgives all mistakes

From raising six children
And trying to work to make ends meet
You show you have endurance
And there's nothing you can't defeat

You are such an example
Of a strong black woman –tough and stern
We could not help as children
But to grasp, listen, look and learn

You taught us independence
You taught us how to love
You taught us patience and understanding
You're the pillar of all above

We thank you for your warmth
And the loving smile you so often give
We thank God for your birthday
Fifty-eight years he's let you live

And we appreciate your dedication
To whatever you partake
We simply cherish your every step
For all the accomplishments you make. . .

A Giving Mother

Are you still a giving mother
As you were while giving birth
Or have you forgotten about the time
When your child had unlimited worth. . ?

Are you still a giving mother
One who talks to her kids
Or have you left it up to the schools
Do you feel your child's a Wiz. . ?

Are you still a giving mother
Or do you try to avoid your child
Do you consider them worrisome
Gone crazy or simply gone hay wild. . ?

Are you still a giving mother
Have you taught your child to pray
Have you gone with them to activities
Have you gone to see them play. . ?

Are you still a giving mother
Do you feel your child owes you
Because of bringing them into this world
Now you feel your job is through. . ?

Are you still a giving mother
Just as God as his son, Jesus Christ
Who was born that we might live
One who paid the highest price. . ?

A Mother's Love

How precious is a love that's sincere
A love that never ends
From the one who brought us here
One so quick to defend

How grateful a child must feel
To be pampered from head to toe
And be supported every day of our lives
No matter how old we grow

How lonely we must be
When hurt, and see no Mother's face
But when alarmed she will appear
No matter where the place

How dedicated is the one
Who'll lay it on the line
When feeling down and out
She'll whisper, "Bless the child of mine."

A Grand Celebration

To: Amandalo Brown
For: Maeida Javonica Brown

For it was he who saw the need
For you to be my mother . . .
The love you've shown since my inception
Has been unlike no other . . .

There has not been a moment that
I've felt I could not call . . .
When I'm aware that you're in need
I will not let you fall . . .

It's not a day that passed by
When you don't cross my mind . . .
I'll be right there when trouble comes
In just a matter of time . . .

For it is he who encourages us
To go on day by day . . .
No matter what the ridicule
No matter what others say . . .

You have learned to live your life
Not letting disappointments get you down . . .
You have learned to wear a smile
When you want to wear a frown . . .

I have learned to respect you
I love and cherish you from my heart . . .
Because of the life we share
Because of the joy you've brought . . .

The celebration hasn't just begun
Nor will it end today . . .
As you keep your hand in the Master's hand
I'll keep kneeling down to pray . . .

Friendship

To: Jelani
Happy Birthday 9/6/02

I feel I've found a friends in you
One whom I can talk with – One
Whom I can depend . . .

I feel I've found some joy with you
For you make me laugh and give
Me a reason to smile . . .

I feel I've found some time with you
Time to rest . . . time to share . . .
Time to listen . . . Time to care . . .

I feel I've opened my book
And have written more pages
Expanded my knowledge and
Accepted my short comings . . .

The Kelley's
James, Valery,
Ja'Va & Christopher

True Friendship

Janet Berry Cole
19-Jan-08

Reflecting on when we first met
And I introduced myself to you . . .
I told you that if you ever needed my help
I'd be a friend that's true . . .

True friendship allows each person
To be their very own . . .
And makes one feel at ease
When they're away from home . . .

A friendship that doesn't crowd you
Pressure of try to corrupt the mind . . .
And allows room for breathing
And withstands the test of time . . .

We've never found the need to argue
And hardly ever disagree . . .
But, respect each other's wishes
No matter what each other may plea . . .

From teenagers to your 50th Birthday
It's still an honor to be your friend . . .
You're a God given blessing and assurance
One whom I feel I can depend . . .

We may not talk everyday
Doesn't matter if the months go by . . .
I know that I can call you
I feel you're hurt when you cry . . .

You're still the same Janet I met
Full of beauty, joy and grace. . .
You'll always remain close to my heart
No matter the situation or the place . . .

Happy Birthday!

This Day

To: Roy Leverette

God let you live to see
A birthday for another year . . .
And he's given you wise counsel
To know that judgement's near . . .

God let you live to fee
His presence and his love . . .
And he gives you perfect peace
Just as his little dove . . .

God let you live to witness
His purpose and his will . . .
And all of his goodness
For your life he shall fill . . .

God let you live to touch
Other hearts that come your way . . .
And he's given you a vision
Through the talents you portray . . .

God let you live for this day
To bless others as he blesses you . . .
And he'll continue to direct
Any circumstance – He'll bring you through . . .

Happy Birthday

"Miss Gillette"

May 25, 2019

You are such an inspiration
You bring joy to all around . . .
We are blessed to have you here
With your mind so sharp and sound . . .

We know that you love plants and flowers
You care for yours everyday . . .
You ensure that they are healthy
In a mother kind of way . . .

We celebrate your 95th Birthday
By expressing how much we care . . .
By coming with food, gifts, prayers and songs
And lots of love is in the air . . .

May God continue to bless you
Be your strength, your Lord and guide . . .
May you keep the will to serve Him
As we watch you with great pride . . .

You usher in the Holy Spirit

You encourage us as you sing . . .

Piney Grove A.M.E Zion Church family and others

Say "Happy Birthday" to your name . . .

Happy Wedding Anniversary

To: Rev. Dr. Robert Little, Jr. & Mrs. Glenda Little

Yes, it was fifty years ago
When Robert and Glenda joined hands...
They vowed to love each other
And always try to understand...

That there will be times
When all would not go well...
And to value each others opinions
Sharing secrets they'd never tell...

As the years have gone by
And children came into play...
Robbie and Regina gives them so much joy
Beyond measure still today...

And now, of course, there are grandchildren
In which they spoil from time to time...
But, always encouraging & supporting them
To do their best and stay in line...

After years in the private sector workforce
They both were able to retire...
And go wholeheartedly into the ministry
Eagerly accepting the calling from on high...

So here they are -Our Pastor and First lady
Their love story continues to unfold...
Happy 50th Wedding Anniversary
Glad you're in the business of saving & winning souls...

------------------------ ------------------------

Happy Birthday, Linda

December 28, 2001

We just wanted to celebrate
Your being another year old . . .
We're sure you have lots of stories to share
Even some you've never told . . .

Since you're half one hundred
And now over the hill . . .
We'll let you take a little time
To be thankful for in the past thrills . . .

We know you still have lots of spunk
And fisty as can be . . .
You still know how to swing a whip
Having us saving, Lord Have Mercy . . .

We are all so grateful
That you were put here on this earth . . .
And God won't let you go out
Since you've accepted his new birth . . .

So, Happy Birthday to YOU
May God bless you with many more . . .
Eat, have fun and remember
That a healing is at his opened door . . .

Happy Birthday

First Lady, Sis. Angela Phillips
From: Eldress Sheryl Smith

God has given you the task

To be by Pastor Phillip's side . . .

To encourage and to support his ministry

To help him lead and guide . . .

God has instilled in you

The will to keep pressing on . . .

To love, to teach, to preach his word

And to be the link that's strong . . .

You are a dynamic, praying woman

With an angelic voice to sing . . .

To speak and let others know

Of the joy that Jesus' brings . . .

So, we celebrate you today

And pray God's blessings upon you, too . . .

For English Chapel is so honored

To have a first lady such as you!

My Relative

For: William "Bill" Godette
Purpose: Birthday Celebration

Not often do I pause to say
How important you are to me
And how my life's been simplied
With raising our family . . .

So right now let me tell you
I couldn't ask for a better man
One who laughs as well as cries
One who shows he understands . . .

And, daddy, we could say the same
There are times we've neglected too
But, deep down in our hearts
We've been so very proud of you . . .

Proud of how you've taught us
To trust God and weight things out
And stand firm in our actions
And not show a trace of doubt . . .

So, Granddaddy - - I'm your heart
You've shown me a lot of fun
I run to you in times of trouble
For your work is never done . . .

We all appreciate who you are to us
As we celebrate with you today
For there is no other relative
That has touched us quite the same way . . .

------------------------------ ------------------------------

Celebration

To: Rev. James Vance
January 24, 2018

A Pastor of such caliber
Is definitely hard to find . . .
Especially one who takes the initiative
To talk to anyone at anytime . . .

It's not like a hop and a skip
From Kinston to Harlowe . . .
But, all we have to do is call
And you'll come unlike no show . . .

Not only can your preach like Paul
Profounding the unadulterated truth . . .
But you reach every man and woman
Not excluding our children and our youth . . .

Not only can you sing like angels
With a voice so powerful, yet sincere . . .
You've helped to lift many burdens
And dry up many tears . . .

Continue to bring the message forth
As we celebrate your being born . . .
Continue to run this Christian Race
Though persecuted, rebuked and scorned . . .

At last, we say "Happy birthday!"
To one who's touched us in many ways . . .
And may God grant you his perfect peace
Until life is over upon this stage . . .

Celebration

To: Frankie Gibbs
7/17/01

A time to really think about
How God has kept you whole. . .
And how it's such a blessing
To one day just behold. . .

Behold the beauty of his face
And thank him for your birth. . .
And express your gratitude
Of days upon this earth. . .

To tell God in your own words
How much he truly means. . .
And what your insides feel like
About the joy that only he brings. . .

So, yes today you celebrate
Your being allowed to live. . .
To witness to those you meet
What knowing Christ can give. . .

HAPPY BIRTHDAY!

Love

Love is the feeling of Joy and Delight . . .
It makes you think all through the night . . .
You wonder what will happen the next day . . .
Will we break up or will things stay okay . . .
I pray and ask God with all my heart . . .
To let us remain together and never depart . . .
Love is to care for someone in need . . .
To never let down to always succeed . . .

Unlimited Love

When a person has done, is doing, does and will do for the other no matter what . . . UNLIMITED LOVE . . . When a person is accepted as they are or changes to better themselves mainly because of the other. . . UNLIMITED LOVE. . .

When a person consults the other before making big decisions or when the partner has faith in what has been decided . . . UNLIMITED LOVE . . .

When a person suffers all day long or will suffer throughout the night to save the other from pain and torment . . . UNLIMITED LOVE . . .

When a person ceases from struggling with their feelings and just dwells on the warmth of their bodies and hearts when the other is nearby or far away . . . UNLIMITED LOVE . . .

When a person knows that they have loved, realizes that they love and is determined even if in doubt to love again . . . UNLIMITED LOVE . . .

Maybe I Am

Maybe I am afraid . . .
- OF YOUR LAUGHTER
- OF YOUR TEARS
- OF YOUR HUGS
- OF YOUR FEARS

Maybe I am afraid . . .
- OF YOUR CLOSENESS
- OF YOUR DISTANCE
- OF YOUR STRAIGHT FORWARDNESS
- OF YOUR IRRESISTANCE

Maybe I am afraid . . .
- OF YOUR EAGERNESS
- OF YOUR YEANING
- OF YOUR DESIRES
- OF YOUR LEARNING

Maybe I am afraid . . .
> OF YOUR DISCIPLINE
> OF YOUR SHARING
> OF YOUR OPENNESS
> OF YOUR CARING

Maybe I am afraid
> TO LOVE YOU

HAPPY BIRTHDAY . . .

While I'm Yours And You Are Mine

With your body real close to mine

Our hearts will always intertwine . . .

No matter how far we are apart

I know I'm carried within your hear . . .

Time will tell how much you care

The fire we make will flow or flare . . .

For I do know you need my touch

And I need yours just as much . . .

Tears may flow from my eyes

If you're an imposter or in disguise . . .

So do not fake, or make believe

And do not cheat, please don't deceive . . .

I'll trust in you and you in me

We'll explore together in ecstasy . . .

Our love will never fade away

If we just believe in what we say . . .

Let us not confuse over with concerned

Nor confuse what we've taught with what we've learned . . .

But, try to gain more knowledge on each

And be right there so I won't have to reach . . .

We're so alike different in some views
But, we'll be okay if neither misuse . . .
No one can tell me that I am blind
Not while I'm yours and you are mine . . .

I Desire A Partner

IT'S IN TIMES OF CRISIS THAT I EXPECT YOUR AVAILABILITY
IN TIMES OF LONELINESS I WANT YOUR ATTENTION
IN TIMES OF DEPRESSION I NEED YOUR SHOULDER
I DESIRE A PARTNER

IT'S IN TIMES LIKE THESE I NEED AFFECTION
IN TIMES OF SICKNESS ASSISTANCE IS NECESSARY
IN TIMES OF TROUBLE YOU COULD HIDE ME
I DESIRE A PARTNER

IT'S IN TIMES LIKE THESE DEVOTION IS REQUIRED
IN TIMES OF FEAR I NEED BRAVERY
IN TIMES OF SADNESS I MAY SEEK SYMPATHY
I DESIRE A PARTNER

IT'S IN TIMES OF DESPAIR I KNOW THERE IS HOPE
IN TIMES OF WEARINESS I SEARCH FOR CONTENTMENT
IN TIMES OF HUNGAR I THIRST FOR FULFILLMENT
I DESIRE A PARTNER

AT THIS TIME IN YOUR LIFE YOU, TOO, LACK SATISFACTION
YOU, TOO, NEED A COMPANION
YOU, TOO WANT WHAT YOU WANT
YOU, TOO, DESIRE A PARTNER. . .

Not One

Not one time have you called
To see if I was okay
To see if I needed anything
To take time with me to pray

Not one time have you visited
No mentioning of your name
Just hoping your vehicle would appear
Was months ago a game. . ?

Not one time have you considered
What's expected of you to do
But, seemingly it doesn't matter
Cause your mission is now though

Not one time have you reflected
On how I now must feel
On how you acted to so sincere
Was anything you claimed for real. . ?

Not one time you must remember
The closeness I thought we shared
The actions of inseparable
That has faded from your cares

Not one time have you offered to come stand by my side
Much unlike when you needed me
You tried daily on me to thribe

Not one time you have attended
To our business left undone
The load is getting might heavy
As though I weigh a ton

My Candy

When you are away from me
I miss you so very much...
I could never verbally describe
How often I want your touch...

Hold me real close, okay
Don't ever let me go...
Cause I've gotten my eyes on you
No other man I know...

When you are sleeping nights
I'm sure you search for me...
Maybe it is in a dream
Or a part of reality...

Let me just have my way
And see you as I wish...
Cause you've become a part of me
The candy in my dish...

Real Close

JUST HOLD ME REAL, REAL, CLOSE
CAN'T YOU FEEL MY NEEDS
JUST TO HOLD ME REAL, REAL CLOSE
CAN'T YOU FEEL MY WANTS
JUST TO HOLD ME REAL, REAL CLOSE
CAN'T YOU FEEL MY HURT
JUST TO HOLD ME REAL, REAL CLOSE
CAN'T YOU FEEL MY FEAR
JUST TO HOLD ME REAL, REAL CLOSE
JUST KISS ME RIGHT NOW. . .

JUST TO HOLD ME REAL, REAL CLOSE
CAN'T YOU FEEL MY JOY
JUST TO HOLD ME REAL, REAL CLOSE
CAN'T YOU FEEL MY PAIN
JUST TO HOLD ME REAL, REAL CLOSE
CAN'T YOU FEEL MY DESIRE
JUST TO HOLD ME REAL, REAL CLOSE
CAN'T YOU FEEL MY ANXIETY
JUST TO HOLD ME REAL, REAL CLOSE
JUST TOUCH ME RIGHT NOW

JUST TO HOLD ME REAL, REAL CLOSE
CAN'T YOU FEEL WHAT I FEEL
JUST TO HOLD ME REAL, REAL CLOSE
CAN'T YOU FEEL MY WARMTH

JUST TO HOLD ME REAL, REAL CLOSE
CAN'T YOU FEEL ME INSIDE
JUST TO HOLD ME REAL, REAL CLOSE
CAN'T YOU FEEL MY CONTENTMENT
JUST TO HOLD ME REAL, REAL CLOSE
JUST DON'T LET ME GO

I Care So Much

You wonder if I love you
I try so hard to explain...
How much I really care for you
And that it's you I claim...

It's hard for me to say those words
They mean so much to me...
When it's meant to be said
I'll express it gently...

If I am forced to say it
It simply won't be true...
I'll be trying to ease my mind
By verbably pleasing you...

Our feelings for each are so deep
You love me oh--so much...
If only I would say the same
You'd demand, expect and such...

Be opened for my opinions
They'll suddenly be released...
I also expect the same from you
Cause my care has increased...

You title it as you please
The word, "LOVE", is too broad for me...
But, I care for you so much
That I can't let go of thee...

God knows how I fell about you
And I've left it in his hands...
To guide me in the right way
And always help me stand...

My heart sometimes ache inside
And tingle when you're near...
You bring out the real in me
You've cast away my fear...

These all may be symptoms of love
Or, so we have been told...
I talk about you all the time
I look at you as gold...

If I had to die for you
I'd do it with a smile...
Because I knew you loved me
And I cared for you awhile...

Hopefully, our relationship will last
For our feelings are sincere
I'll continue to call you my guy
As you call me your dear...

Let her show you the time you've longed to be shown...
Let her touch you the way you've never even known...
Let her feel the warmth of your body to hers...
You can both exemplify the bees and the birds...

Let her examine a bit of your love...
Let her be below and you be above...
Let her smell the air that you breath...
Together you'll feel the other ones needs...

Let her bring happiness into your life...
Let her today know she is your wife...
Let her always believe that you're number one...
You two, together, show the meaning of fun...

Let her gain confidence in you as a man...
Let her have no need to survey the land...
Let her know, not think all the time...
That there's always thick, never thin line...

Let her speak when she wants to be heard...
Let her cease when she seems without words...
Let her be the women who'll fight for her rights...
A massage will ease her pains in the night...

Let her gently rub around your hairy chest...
Let her feel your head rest against her breast...
Let her have no doubt that you exist...
Show loving you is never a risk...

Let her never feel unwanted or ashamed...
Let her be proud to speak of your name...
Let her climb the mountains and cross many creeks...
Never leave her alone for months or for weeks...

Let her taste the honey in your cup...
Let her know never to give you up...
I wanna know how it will be...
If you've decided and willing to let her be ME...

My Life

To: Thomas Price

OH DADDY, WHY DID YOU LEAVE US
ALONE TO CRAWL, TO GROW, TO LIVE..?
IF ONLY YOU WOULD'VE EXPLAINED TO MOM
I'D BETTER UNDERSTAND THE WHOLE ORDEAL...

OH NAVY, THANKS FOR THE TRAINING
THE DISCIPLINE IF YOU WILL...
SOMETHING I SHALL CHERISH
THAT I CONSTANTLY THINK OF STILL...

THE WATERS CHILLED MY BODY
THE SHIPS WERE STERN AND TOUGH...
THE FELLOWSHIP, HOW TREMENDOUS
BUT WAS THE NAVY ENOUGH...?

I'VE HAD A LOT OF TRADES
ONE QUICKLY COMES TO MIND...
OH, IF I COULD JUST GO BACK
I'D CHANGE THE HANDS OF TIME...

IF I COULD PEEP AT THE HOLE CARD
AND HAVE KNOWN WHAT I KNOW NOW...
I'D THROW MY HANDS UP TO THE SKY
AND ASK MYSELF "How"..?

IF I COULD SAIL THE SEA AGAIN
AND FLOAT UPON SOME SHORE...
I'D CHOOSE THE ISLAND NEAREST HOME
AND BE CONTENT FOREVERMORE...

I REALLY LOVED MY FIRST WIFE
FROM THIS UNION TWO WERE BORN...
MY DAUGHTERS ARE SWEET DARLINGS
ONE OF WHICH HAD ALREADY JOINED...

JOINED INTO THE MARRIAGE CIRCLE
THAT I DO NOT NOW PARTAKE...
CAUSE MY SECOND WIFE WAS CO-DEPENDENT
ON EVERY EARNING I COULD MAKE...

TWO MORE GIRLS WERE BORN THE SECOND TIME
THEY ARE PRECIOUS AND SO PURE...
I SEE THEM AS OFTEN AS I CAN
MY LOVE FOR THEM IS SO SECURE...

YES, I WAS ROBBED OF MY INDEPENDENCE
THAT I ALLOWED TO GIVE AWAY...
WHY I WENT THROUGH ALLL THOSE CHANGES
I STILL QUESTION IT TODAY...

I LEARNED NOT TO PUT MY TRUST IN HUMAN
BUT, TO PUT MY FAITH IN GOD...
FOR SOME I ACT STRANGE
AND TO OTHERS I AM ODD....

I WAS LIVING IN CONTINUATION
SOMEONE RELYING ON JUST ME...
I'M SO GLAD THAT THE ACT IS OVER
AND RIGHT NOW I FEEL SO FREE...

I CHOOSE NOT TO REPORT
OR HAVE SOMEONE HANGING AROUND...
WAITING FOR ME TO COME HOME
AND TO GREET ME WITH A FROWN...

I'M SO THANKFUL FOR MY HORSES
THEY BRING ME JOY WHEN I'M DEPRESSED...
AND THEY MAKE ME FEEL SO PROUD
THEY RELEASE ME WHEN I AM STRESSED...

OH, I THANK DEAR GOD FOR MOMMA
SHE IS SUCH AS JEWEL TO ME...
WE'RE WHAT'S LEFT IN OUR IMMEDIATE FAMILY
ONCE WAS BLIND, BUT NOW I SEE...

YES, IT'S GOD'S AMAZING GRACE
THAT HAS BROUGHT ME SAFE THUS FAR...
I ACCEPT HIS CLEANSING POWER
IT'S PROVEN GREATER THAN THE BAR...

Class Reunion

To: Thomas Freddie Price

It was many, many, moons ago
Thirty-Five to be exact...
When we roamed the halls of Green Central High
Not knowing today how we'd react...

To seeing our many classmates
And reminiscencing of our past...
Sharing memories and renewing friendships
Seeing old loves that did not last...

It is so exciting
To see who married who...
And who has the most children
Or a notable job or two...

And what about grandchildren
And who's been married the most...
Is anyone now preaching
Or a famous talk show host..?

Are there any politicians
Employees of the State or Government..?
Anyone feeling down on themselves
Due to a life not well spent..?

Well, I'm sure that all expressions
Will come to each of our minds...
Reunions help us realize
That our destiny's have set times...

So, let's enjoy each other
Cry, laugh and just have fun. . .
Leave her feeling rejuvenated
When all is said and done. . .

I Knew It, Had To Be You

For: Nichelle Becton's Wedding

YOU SOMEHOW MAKE ME FEEL BRAND NEW
WE'D BECOME SO CLOSE AT HEART
NOTHING COULD SEEMINGLY KEEP US APART
I KNEW IT HAD TO BE YOU...

PHYSICALLY AND EDUCATIONALLY I'VE GROWN
YOU'VE ACCEPTED WELL ALL OF MY FAULTS
ALTHOUGH AT TIMES YOU, TOO, HAVE FALLEN SHORT
YOU'RE THE KINDEST OF MEN I'VE KNOWN...

THERE WERE TIMES WE COULD'VE CALLED IT QUITS
INSTEAD WITH GOD WE WORKED THINGS OUT
WITH LOTS OF SUNSHINE WITHOUT A SHADOW OF DOUBT
I BELIEVE THAT WE CAN MAKE IT...

MY MIND IS SET TO DO MY PART
RESPONSIBILITIES, I'M GAIN TO SHARE
KNOWING HOW WE BOTH REALLY CARE
WE'RE OFF TO A REALLY GREAT START...

NOW I MAKE MY DEVOTED VOW
TO HONOR, TO LOVE, AND RESPECT
THE SAME VIBES FROM YOU, I DETECT
IT'S YOU AND ME NOW........

---------------------- ----------------------

To Have And To Hold

My vow is to have you and you only
To hold you for the rest of my life til death us do part. . .
And not dwell on if's and but's from the start
Just to have and to hold. . .

My vow is to add your happiness
Subtract any doubt of unfaithfulness. . .
Be straightforward and forever grateful
Just to have and to hold. . .

My vow is to keep an understanding mind
Give willingly as well as take unselfishly. . .
Be real and honest as should be
Just to have and to hold. . .

My vow is to honor and to cherish
Acknowledge the unpleasant and praise the adorable. . .
Recognize the outragous and attend the affordable
Just to have and to hold. . .

My vow is to elaborate on positiveness
Stay structured on concrete stability. . .
Never underminding our decisions or abilities
Just to have and to hold. . .

My vow is to accept and appreciate our love
Remain connected from the heart, body and mind. . .
Whatever else is needed, Let us define
Right now, I feel privileged just to have and to hold. . .

You Are Complete

To: Shantel Godette

WHAT GOD HAS JOINED TOGETHER
NO MAN CAN SEPARATE
NO MATTER WHAT IS SAID OR DONE
NO MATTER ABOUT MISTAKES

WITH GOD AS THE WITNESS
FOR WHAT HAS BEEN APPROVED
NO ONE CAN ENTER IN BETWEEN
AND CAUSE YOUR BATTLE LOSE

THE WAY GETS ROUGH, YET EASY
AS YOU DESIRE WHAT LIES AHEAD
IT WILL SOB ON ROCK BOTTOM
IF CHRIST IS NOT THE BREAD

SHANTEL AND ISAIAH
SOMETIMES YOU'RE CHALLENGED WITH NO RECEIPT
FRAGMENTS MAY BE IN THE MIDST
BUT, RIGHT NOW, YOU ARE COMPLETE. . .

My Baby Brother, Freddie

To: Clarence Earl Fisher
10/1/10

There's no one like a brother
Who's close to your heart. . .
Nothing like the pain you feel
When either has to part. . .

So glad I went to see him
Just before God called him home. . .
And that we had a close relationship
God knows how now I feel alone. . .

There is simply an emptiness
A void that cannot be filled. . .
I cherish our intimate conservations
And the very life he lived. . .

I do not have to worry
Whether he was right with Christ. . .
Because I know he knew his maker
And his ultimate sacrifice. . .

I may appear sad from the outside
Deep down inside I'm overjoyed. . .
I just miss my baby brother
Yet, I'm rejoicing in the Lord!

Life For Me

To: Freddie

LIFE FOR ME HAS NOT BEEN EASY
AND IT'S PARTIALLY MY FAULT. . .
SEEMS I'VE ALTERED FROM HIS PLAN
NOT ALWAYS DOING AS I OUGHT. . .

I KNOW MY LIFE HAS BEEN ANCHORED
AND GOD CARES FOR WHAT I DO. . .
CAUSE HE'S BROUGHT ME TO THE LIGHT
AND TODAY I FEEL BRAND NEW. . .

LIFE FOR ME HAS BEEN A CHALLENGE
THAT I'VE FACED FROM DAY TO DAY. . .
I'M SO GRATEFUL TO GOD ALMIGHTY
FOR REMINDING ME OF THE PRICE HE PAID. . .

KEEPING THIS IN MIND HELPS ME
TO ACCEPT APART FROM THE CHANGE. . .
CAUSE I'VE MOVED FROM PLACE TO PLACE
YET, I'VE FOUND HOME ON THE RANGE. . .

LIFE FOR ME HAS BEEN ROSES
AS COMPARED TO OTHERS AROUND. . .
SO, HOW AND WHY SHOULD I COMPLAIN
I LOOK UP WHILE OTHERS DOWN. . .

I HAVE LEARNED TO TAKE LIFE EASY
AND NOT TAKE EVERYTHING AT HEART...
I NOW LOOK OUT FOR NUMBER ONE
AS I SHOULD HAVE FROM THE START...

I HAVE LED AND FOLLOWED SAMPLE
OF WHAT GOD AND OTHERS STRESS...
MY TODAY IS WHAT I MAKE IT
I'M NOW GEARED UP FOR SUCCESS...

We Were There

We were there to witness your health
There when your health declined. . .
We wanted so bad to make you stay
God had something else in mind. . .

We've practiced your suggestions
Of how we ought to be. . .
But, now you've gone to Glory
To spend Eternity. . .

Oh Granddaddy, don't you worry
About the family left behind. . .
Cause God has it in control
It's peace in him we'll find. . .

We'll take care of your daughters
And care of your son. . .
We're happy that your pain is over
For now your work is done. . .

Our Neighbors, Our Friend

The funeral of Sarah Frances Fenner
8/31/10

As I look across the field
I'm reminded of several things. . .
How you kept the yard so beautiful
And you kept the house so clean. . .

I'm reminded of your sandwiches
Oh, they smelt so very good. . .
The chicken was so awesome
You asked, Want some pork chops?
Sarah, now you knew we would. . .

In the summers we'd go crabbing
Hattie would fry or stew crabs just right
And when we'd come to visit
We best have an appetite. . .

Ms. Bertha would be sitting there
And Ishman standing at glance. . .
And BA -Somewhere washing a car
Always neat with a crease in his shirt & pants. . .

When you play your music cloud
Dee would head on over across the field. . .
You, two, were just like sisters
Yes, the good times of singing & cutting up was for real. . .

Then came your daughter, Aretha
She was the apple of your eye. . .
We knew that when she was called away
Deep down inside you died. . .

As sickness came upon you
When you moved- You were surely missed. . .
Now your smile and laughter's with Jesus
As we salute you with a Kiss. . .

On Behalf of the Neighbors,
The Frazier's, The Carter's
& The Fisher Families

Cousin Joe

To: The Carter Family
11/08/11

We know that you're the last to leave
You hung on so very long. . .
We do not have to worry
Cause your heart was where it belonged. . .
Oh Master, take care of Cousin Joe
And keep him by the sea. . .
Because he loved the waterfront
It made him so happy. . .
We know you loved your family
Your wife, your children and grand's. . .
Didn't have to wonder about his thought
Cousin Joe would take a stand. . .
And we all know that Hazel
Was his favorite cousin of all. . .
It's our belief that when she went on home
God Said, "Joe, Get ready for your call"!
And when the Master called him
He said, "Hazel, I, too am now free . . .
I will see you on your Birthday
And you can celebrate with me. . .

Safe In His Arms

To: Family of Thomas Lee "Tommy" Brown Moore
7/25/1945-/18/2011
1st Cousin 5/29/11
The Omega Protein Inc. pogy fishing boat "Sandy Point"

You wonndered if I had made it

Yes, I helped save the rest. . .

I tried to get up out of the boat

But, God truly knows what's best. . .

He said, "You're a great swimmer"

And such an exceptional man. . .

You're always there for others

I need you, Now, in my plan. . .

I know the wates were raging

Yet, I heard the sounding alarm. . .

I alerted the other fishermen

Praying that they were free from harm. . .

You must not feel your dreams are shattered

You were shown where I would be. . .

There is peace just in knowing

God's plan to rescue me. . .

For you who do not know the Christ

May not accept and question why?
For I've gone to meet my maker
In the land beyond the sky...
I am Safe in HIS arms
Although your tear drops may fall...
Try living the life worth living
So you, too, can answer the Master's Call...

Retirement / Work

Happy Retirement

From: Your employees of FSC
To: Donnie Parrott
9/13/12

It seems like just yesterday

When you arrived on the scene. . .

So many of us were just days apart

From joining this domain. . .

As the years have gone by

We've seen many come and go. . .

And we've seen the spirits of many

Darken as well as glow. . .

On this day your heart must shine

We know it's bitter/sweet. . .

Go for a boat ride or sit in your recliner

Lay back and prop up your feet. . .

We know it's your time to build

More houses & boats to name a few. . .

It's awesome that you have

The talents that you do. . .

So, today we say "Happy Retirement"
We will miss from hearing your name. . .
And know that Good ole FSC
Will never be the same. . .

Retirement Celebration

For: Albert Toon

YOUR LENGTH OF SERVICE HAS CONCLUDED
YOUR TIME IN THE ARMY RESERVES NOW ENDS...
IT'S TIME TO RELAX AND DO WHAT YOU WANT
SHARE TIME AS YOU CHOOSE TO SPEND...
IT'S TIME TO CELEBRATE THE FORTY YEARS
YOU DECIDED TO TAKE DIRECTION...
AND SHARE WITH FRIENDS AND FAMILY
THE DIFFICULT TIMES OF MEETING INSPECTIONS...
THERE MAY HAVE BEEN SOME CHALLENGES
THAT WERE NOT ALWAYS MET...
BUT, IT IS EVIDENT THAT THE TRAINING
SURELY PREPARED YOU TO PROTECT...
RIGHT NOW YOU SHOULD PAUSE TO REFLECT
ON THE EXCITEMENT, THE JOY AND PAIN...
YOU'RE AN EXAMPLE TO MANY OTHERS
WHOSE AMBITION INCLUDES TO GAIN...
FOR YOU'VE SHOWN THAT YOU'RE DILIGENT
BY ATTENDING CAMP AS IT'S ASSIGNED...
AND BY SUPPORTING THE ENTIRE FAMILY
AS A HUSBAND AND FATHER IS DEFINED...

SO, TODAY WE LIFT OUR HATS
WE SALUTE IN GRANDEST STYLE...
FOR TO US YOU ARE THE GREATEST
CAUSE YOU'VE GONE THE EXTRA MILE...
FOR WE KNOW WE NEED NOT WORRY
THAT YOU'LL SIT DOWN AND FALL APART...
BECAUSE YOU'RE INVOLVED IN MANY ACTIVITES
THAT YOU TAKE CLOSE TO YOUR HEART...
SO, CONGRATULATIONS FOR ALL OF US
HEAVY BOAT TRANSPORTATION WILL NOT BE THE SAME...
EVERY NOW AND THEN WE BELIEVE
THEY'LL BE MENTIONING YOUR NAME...

------------------- -------------------

Happy Retirement

To: Candy Hill
September 29, 2011

It has truly been a pleasure

Working with you in FSC...

Don't know how I would have made it

Had you not been there for me...

The "QA" Program was your baby

With your wisdom it was designed...

As you let go and turn it over

Know that things will work out fine...

Cindy and I will do our best

To keep the program second to none...

Days of laughter will continue

As we work hard, yet still have fun...

You relax and enjoy retirement

Take life easy and travel around...

I know that you'll keep busy

With all the many hobbies you've found. . .

Please come back and visit our office

And keep close in touch

Know that you have made a difference

And will be missed very much. . .

Safe in His Arms

To: Will Wallain 2/12/09

It seems like just days ago

You accepted a job at FSC...

You & Donnie joined Bill & Johnny

And it became on big Family...

Some other folk were in the midst

And others were anxious a part...

Like Richard, Vince, Leo & Ronnie

And Charlie kept things in order from the start...

Let's not forget Anita, Jeff & Freddie

Who exist on this earth no more...

What about Nita getting in it with Joe

Grabbing her mess and rushing out the door!!!

When we think of accross the street

Debbie, Doris and Specialist June Finn...

Didn't she have her stuff together

And a fighter right until the end? ? ?

Well, all that was in our past

Now, the future is at stake...

You're moving on to higher grounds

And HUD definitely didn't make a mistake...

You go on and do your best. . .

Think of Candy, Cindy, Connie & Mike. . .

Ancil, Kelly, Rick, Lundy & Billy. . .

Wayne, Richard & now Donnie leading this flight. . .

So, as you fly in the near future

Inspecting construction sites here & there. . .

May the Lord keep you & Sarah

Safe in his arms & in his care. . .

Farewell

For Cherry Point your days are numbered

You're moving on to a more challenging field. . .

Where you'll have to travel making HUD inspections

Just as your ex-coworker, Will. . .

We know your work ethics are superior

We rate your attention to detail second to none. . .

We hope you'll sometimes stop for pleasure

When you know your projects are done. . .

Thinking back on FSC

Your being there from the start. . .

We can understand your frustrations

And how your actions come from your heart. . .

You wanted documentations to be. . .

There were no in between. . .

We'd even go a little further and say

You made Contractor's reporting easier to explain. . .

Being Inspector's of various Contracts

We all share expressions alike. . .

As long as the outcome is satisfactory

Your baby was Asbestos, you handled it right. . .

Charlie Debrul was the 1st Supervisor

You were on the Inspector's list. . .

With Bill, Johnnie, Jeff, Richard and Leo

We all had our share of shifts. . .

Ronnie, Anita, Wayne, Donnie, & Will came along

Debbie Lewellen, there from the start. . .

Trying hard to make end meet

Our section has never grown apart. . .

Freddie, Joe, Scott, Cindy, & Mary

Nancy, Top, Liner, to name some more. . .

Oh, what about extrapolation

And the Daily Reports galore. . .

Now there's Connie, Kelly & Billy

Ancil, Mike, Lundy, and Rick here to explore

Candy, Cindy & myself in QA

And Donnie leading us to heights much more. . .

At FSC

IT STARTED BACK SOME YEARS AGO
WITH CHARLIE AS MY BOSS...
AND ANITA WAS MY PARTNER
WHOSE DEATH WAS A TRAGIC LOSS...
YES, THE YEARS HAVE GONE BY
AND THE ADMINISTRATION HAS CHANGED...
SO MANY HAVE COME AND GONE
FAR TOO MANY TO BEGIN TO NAME...
LOOKING OVER THE ROOM TODAY
LOTS OF EMPLOYEE'S ARE STILL CARRYING ON...
AND I KNOW YOU SHALL REMAIN HERE
TO HELP TO WEATHER THE STORM...
LINDA AND RONNIE CONTINUE
TO BE THE PEOPLE
THAT I HAVE FOUND YOU TO BE...
BEING KIND IN EVERY ACTION
BUT, YET TACTFUL WHEN THERE'S A NEED...
FOR ALL THE REST THAT I'VE ENCOUNTERED
WHOM I HAVE WORKED WITH
THROUGH THE YEARS...
I'LL NOT SAY GOOD-BYE, BUT GOD BLESS YOU
NOW LIFT YOUR GLASS FOR HAPPY CHEERS...

Happy Retirement

To: Danny Skinner

Some relationships are lasting

And it's hard to realize. . .

That's you're retiring from FMD

And we're saying our goodbye's. . .

Your fussing must continue

Our inspecting now must end. . .

We appreciate your maintenance wisdom

Now your new job must begin. . .

But when coworkers really connect

No matter how far we are part. . .

There will always be a spot

Of your remembrance in our hearts. . .

From: Quality Assurance Specialist:

Candy Hill

Cynthia Jones

Valery Kelley

Doing Your Thing

To: M. Wayne Walter
From: Co-workers of FSC
December 19, 2012

It is such a blesssing

That you're retiring from FSC

There have been lots of changes

Same old, same old, we'll never see...

Just think of the bright side

As we reflect on your journey thus far...

From being called a QAE and CSR

And now classified as a PAR...

You have reached another milestone

And your time here is near complete...

Your years with the Federal Government

Is time that definitely can not be beat...

So, enjoy being in your work shed

Making the leather work for you...

And traveling around the world

Enjoying the wonderful things you do...

Take your Harley on a joy ride

Ride with Sandy on your side...

And enjoy your bug & little grands
Who have brought you so much pride. . .
We will miss your debates & discussions
Your opinions & other things. . .
But, we will spread the great news
As you continue to spread your wings. . .

------------------------ ------------------------

Retirement Celebration

To: Jamie Colaw
3/30/99

WE REALIZE THAT YOUR WORKING YEARS
HAVEN'T BEEN ALL PEACHES AND CREAM...
SOME DAYS HAVE BEEN FULL OF LAUGHTER
OTHER DAYS YOU JUST COULD SCREAM...
WE KNOW THAT AFTER OVER 29 YEARS
OF WORKING TO SEE THIS DAY...
YOU LOOK BACK AND SAY TO YOURSELF
IT REALLY HAS BEEN OKAY...
FROM A CLERK TYPIST TO STENO TYPIST
TO DISTRIBUTING CLERK AND AT LAST...
A CREDIT CARD COORDINATOR WILL ALL
SOON BE A PART OF YOUR PAST...
A PAST IN WHICH WE CELEBRATE
A PAST IN WHICH WE'RE PROUD...
TO HAVE BEEN A PART OF
THE STEADY TRAVELING CROWD...
NOW, YOU CAN REALLY TRAVEL
AT ANYTIME IN WHICH YOU CHOOSE...
JUST KEEP GOD AS YOUR CO-PILOT

AND TURN THAT TIME CLOCK OFF SNOOZE...
BELIEVE US WHEN WE SAY
YOUR WORK WAS NOT IN VAIN...
SOME WE'LL GIVE TO MANGERIAL ACCOUNTING
AND THE REST TO MIKE FAIN...
CONTINUE YOUR PAST TIME ACTIVITIES
SUCH AS BOWLING AND RIVERDANCE...
AND COME BACK BY TO SEE US
WHENEVER YOU GET A CHANCE...
ENJOY ROGER, BOBBY, AND JENNIE
AND OF COURSE DAVID AND ASHLEY...
CONTINUE TO BE STRONG SUPPORTER
OF YOUR IMMEDIATE FAMILY...
SO, FROM THE COMPTROLLER DEPARTMENT
AND OTHERS GATHERED IN THIS PLACE...
MAY YOU HAVE A JOYOUS RETIREMENT
AND REMAIN FOREVER IN GOD'S GRACE...

On Your Retirement

To: Bruce Wood
Decemeber 15, 1999

TIME TO SIT BACK JUST ROCK OR DECLINE

AND DO THOSE THINGS PLEASING TO YOU...

TRAVEL - - GO SAILING - - PLAY GOLF - - SWING A BAT

PERHAPS DRIBBLE A BALL OR TWO...

WHEN YOU BEGIN TO REMINISCE

ON THE MANY JOBS THAT YOU HAVE HELD...

TO RETIRE AS CHERRY POINT'S COMPTROLLER

I'D SAY YOU'VE DONE VERY WELL...

NOT MANY HAVE REACHED THE LEVEL YOU'VE REACHED

AND HAVE ACCOMPLISHED SUCH MENTIONABLE GOALS...

AND BY YOU HAVING YOUR HEALTH AND STRENGTH

WHO KNOWS WHAT THE FUTURE HOLDS...

WE WERE BLESSED TO HAVE YOU THIRTEEN YEARS

WITH YOUR TIMELY KNOWLEDGE AND SKILLS...

NOW THAT THIS CHALLENGE HAS COME TO AN END

GET OUT THOSE RODS AND REELS...

JUST LET US SHOWER YOU NOW
SPEND QUALITY TIME WITH FAMILY AND FRIENDS...
AND ALWAYS KNOW DOWN IN YOUR HEARTS
WE'LL MISS YOU DEEP DOWN WITHIN...
MAY YOUR DAYS AHEAD BE GOVERNED
BY THE SPIRIT FROM ON HIGH...
AND WHATEVER GOALS YOU'VE SET TO REACH
BE ACCOMPLISHED BY AND BY...

My Retirement

3/1/2018

I am so forever grateful

That I lived to see this day. . .

And that you took the time

To share with me in some way. . .

Not just for today's event

But the others down thru the years. . .

It's hard to just keep a smile

And not shed a few tears. . .

Thank you for your advice, love and support

As I bid farewell to all. . .

Your working with me and sharing life stories

Gave me the greatest gift of all. . .

I will continue to be of service

As I pray the very best for you. . .

Just let God direct your paths

And you'll reach retirement too!

Religious

The Woman's Plight

From the Rib of Man
God saw the need
That the woman be made
One special breed ...

Made into life
To endure some pain . .
Knowing all's worthwhile
If seeking heaven's gain

One of our stated task
To be help meat to man
To join in with him
In fulfilling God's plan

Doing it with obedience
To love, honor and obey
This can truly be accomplished
If the man's in God's stay

As a wife, or a mother
Or a compassionate friend
The instincts of a woman
Are hard to comprehend

As respect is given
Should it be received
The dedication of a faithful woman
Is hard to achieve

Today, we rise to the occasion
Fulfilling spiritual and financial needs
What we undertake is with assurance
Knowing our God will be pleased

For : Women's day '99
Piney Grove A.M.E
Zion Church

God Knew

To: Beverly

God knew I needed someone like you
To enter into my life . . .
To share my inner most secrets
And help ease my trouble and strife . . .

Someone who I could counsel
And give my best advice . . .
Someone who'd be there for me
And I not have to think about it twice . . .

God knew I needed someone
And that you needed me . . .
To make you smile-feel good inside
And explore the same estacy . . .

Someone who would be honest
Who makes God their number one . . .
And who I know strives for the best
In all the efforts they've done . . .

God knew I needed someone
Whose heart would beat as mine . . .
One who'd agree to commitment
Inspite of my conditions at this time . . .

God is Good

To: Reverend Larry Murphy
10-15-98

It's often said that God is good
And I know it for myself . . .
Think of how he died upon that cross
And the testimony that he left . . .

Nothing that does on can hinder us
Cause we are in his care . . .
Doesn't matter how man treats us
Whether or not we feel it's fair . . .

For judgement day is coming
And our hearts must be in tune . . .
We don't want to be left behind
Dancing to the rhythm of unknown . . .

Now let's be a good example
Of a Christian's life well spent . . .
Let's not dwell on worldly things
Or do something to later resent . . .

I Wonder, Yet, I Know

I wonder what we would have done
Had God not sent his only son
To die for since he knew we'd bear
Oh – just take matters to God in prayer

I wonder what we would have said
Had Jesus not bruised, suffered and bled
Way out on a lonely hill
My God must have whispered "Peace be still"

I wonder what we would have sighed
Had we truly witnessed the life denied
Oh – the life given just for me and you
But brothers and sisters what do we do?

I know that he heals our torn hearts
I know that he straightens our crooked walks
I know that the savior lives today
My soul rejoices in a triumphant way

Peace On Earth

12/07/00

It's that time of the year
When love and cheer is spread . . .
When pies and cakes and candles
Are made along with breads . . .

It's the time to give a gift
And be thoughtful of those around . . .
And to witness excitement in the eyes
When snow lies upon the ground . . .

It's the time of the year
To sing those songs of joy . . .
To express our gratitude
With kind words or a thoughtful joy . . .

It's that time of the year
To think of Jesus' birth . . .
And how he sends his angels
To give us Peace on Earth . . .

------------------------ ------------------------

This Time

December 20, 2001

There are so many expressions shown and given
At this time of the year . . .
For some it's smiles and laughter
For other it's sad memories and tears . . .

Tears of losing their loved one
Including the tragedies that September 11th brought . . .
Which opened many of our eyes
To do more as we ought . . .

Our jobs are so valuable
And our expertise even the more . . .
Manufacturing aircraft engine components
To assist with the ongoing war . . .

So, yes there are reasons to celebrate
Our blessed Savior's birth . . .
And the need for continued striving
For peace upon this earth . . .

Much Appreciative

To: Rev. Shawn Williams
From: The Deaconess Board
Piney Grove A.M.E. Zion church
North Harlowe Community

We are all so grateful

That you kept us in mind . . .

You accepted our appointment

And got to Piney Grove on time . . .

There's nothing any greater

What joy to have one our own . . .

To come back to the sanctuary

In which years ago you called your home . . .

Your message blessed our souls

The Church was really on fire . . .

The singing was fantastic

God really satisfied our desires . . .

We are much appreciative
And thankful for the joy you share . . .
Thank God for granting your traveling mercy
And Favor while in Fair Promises' care . . .

Touch Not

To: Debra Bell

Touch not the Anointed one
Whom God has given favor . . .
To go and spread the good news
About Jesus Christ our savior . . .

Touch not the Anointed one
So full of love and desire . . .
So full of the perfect peace
To share with other flames of fire . . .

Touch not the Anointed one . . .
Who's been humbled from on high . . .
So surrounded by the angels
Wings outstretched and opened wide . . .

Touch not the Anointed one
Whom the Lord has given grace . . .
To uplift the low in spirit
To someday behold his face . . .

Social

The Wants of Freedom

Inspired by "Roots"
1977

Do you know what it is to be free white man

Do you truly, yes really understand...

That we, you call Nigger, have really worked hard

And have come a long way with the help of our Lord...?

Do you know what it is to cry a real tear

To beg, yes beg to have your family near...

And if and when they're taken away

Too bad for you they've gone to stay..?

Do you know what it is to be dragged in the dirt

To be beat and whipped and down right hurt...

And made to get down on your knees... And told not to get up until you say please..?

Do you know what it is to care for a man

Without having to hold your owner's hand... To have a child by the one you hate

And not a choice of who to date..?

Do you know what it is to work all day

Barely eat or sleep and gain no pay...

To be spit upon and nothing you could do

But, say to yourself, I'll never forget you..?

Do you know what it is to stand on a stage

And the people around you look with amaze...

While they're raising the prices higher and higher

And the parents still living wondering
which one will buy ya..?

Do you know what it is to be slapped in the face

To be laughed at, talked about because of your
race..To be let down of a job you know you

could hold

Because of the tales the white man told..?

Do you know what it is to be hanged on a tree

And your family standing around in agony...

To be shot down for speaking your peace

And shoved around like a dog on a leash..?

Do you know how it feels just to say, I'm free

And to thank God for ending the misery...

Of slavery times of hard despair

And times when no one seemed to care..?

Give Me Credit

When I have done what you couldn't do. . .
Or when I've accomplished what you wanted. . .
Give me the praise that I deserve. . .
Speak out, and let your voice be heard. . .

When I have walked as far as I can. . .
To reach the other side of land. . .
Be there to welcome me ashore. . .
Be there as you were there before. . .

When I have called your name out loud. . .
Whether I am ashamed or if I'm proud. . .
Let me first have my say. . .
Afterwards, you can leave or stay. . .

When I have cried till tears won't come. . .
Or when I laugh with serious ones. . .
I have a reason for the way I act. . .
Whether to be calm or to distract. . .

So, when my days on Earth are through. . .
I want to be among the few. . .
Who need not say what they were into. . .
But were given credit where credit was due. . .

Parts of Me

I have a mind which I shall use. . .

To make my choice to do or refuse. . .

You can not make me fall your way. . .

If I have no feelings on what you say. . .

My heart is soft, but can be strong. . .

Especially when you're done me wrong. . .

So do not take a piece of it. . .

Until you feel for me a little bit. . .

My knees may ache when I feel weak. . .

Therefore, you must stand near my feet. . .

In case I fall, you'll help me stand. . .

If you are what you say "a man". . .

Don't think you know me by my eyes. . .

For I can fool, I can disguise. . .

I may look as though I care. . .

And you'll feel so just by my stare. . .

My mouth brings out the real in me. . .

When I wanna talk, it just runs free. . .

If I shut up for a minute or two. . .

One reason's because I'm tickled at you. . .

These parts of me, you cannot take. . .

Because they're mine, for Heaven's sake. . .

Death

See Ya Later...... Uncle Buddy

SOMETIMES IT'S HARD TO VISUALIZE
A LOVED ONE LEAVING HERE...
AND OFTEN TIMES IMPOSSIBLE
NOT TO SHED A TEAR...
ALTHOUGH THEY MAY HAVE LIVED A LIFE
ACCORDING TO GOD'S WORD...
IT'S STILL HARD TO ACCEPT THE FACT
WHEN DEATH BELLS ARE HEARD...
BUT, WHAT WE KNOW MOST OF ALL
IS. . WE, TOO, MUST MEET THE MAN...
WHO KNOWS THE MOMENT
OF OUR LAST BREATH
WHO COMFORTS......WHO UNDERSTANDS....

VALERY FRAZIER KELLEY
GREAT NIECE

My Grandma

In memory of Nettie Morris Carter

It's difficult to measure love
Or know what a person may reveal...
About someone they loved so much
Whose voice long ago was stilled...
It was so overwhelming
To the porch out I ran...
To let Mother know that you had died
And crossed over to a fairer land...
I know that I cried for days
And that my heart was broken into...
I so often needed your guidance
But, I could not call on you...
You taught me to rely on Jesus
To let him be my strength and shield...
There are crops being produced
Such as soya beans in our nearby fields...
I know that you're looking down
From your mansion beyond the sky...
I will keep my hands in God's hands
Till I meet you there on high...

---------------------- ----------------------

You're Alright Now

For: Sirrom Tyrrell Williams
Memorial Service: 12/19/20

It was just a few months ago

I peeped into my guest room...

To check on you as you slept

Saying, "Look at my nephew Sirrom"...

It felt so good to have you come

To spend some time with us...

And now I wonder, yet I know

It's in God's hands we trust...

When born you were a butterball

No trouble did you give...

You've always been beyond your years

With such style and zeal to live...

Your sayings must be mentioned

Like, "over yonder, where is that"...

Uncle Jr gave you a quarter for singing

"There Is Hope" at Piney Grove way back...

That encouraged your desire to sing

And spread God's word thru songs...

And be the life of any party

Yet know to whom you belong...
Throughout all your school years
You perfected like we knew you could...
And decided to follow my footsteps
While at FSU, like I figured you would...
The Gospel Choir to Homecoming King
You made your Marks so high...
To becoming an Alpha, yes, first in line
When performing, none could pass you by...
You have left such an impact
On our families, Churches and friends...
We are witnesses that you served God
And had strong faith unto the end...
Our celebrations will not be the same
You're not here to help us plan...
But, your spirit will carry us through
As we journey holding your hand...
Keep on watching over us
We all believe "You're Alright Now"...
As usual, we say your work is superb
So Sirrom, just take your bow...
Bow down before the Almighty King

Get your robe and starry crown...
We can feel your everlasting presence
With God's Angels all around...

I Love You!
Always in my heart,
Aunt Valery

Missing Grandma

In Memory of Nettie Morris Carter
08/06/1910 - 08/20/1979

Lord, you know my heart aches

Thinking of someone I loved so dear...

The one who cultivated my actions

And taught me only you to fear...

Lord, you know my sadness

When thinking of Grandma that she died...

That was such an unforgettable day

I just cried and cried and cried...

I think back on the small things

That became larger as I grew...

And the talks that we shared

That only she and I knew...

I remember that she loved coffee

And Sanka was her choice...

And that no one else was in charge

Because Grandma was the boss...

She loved to cook apple dumplings
Gingerbread cake, pineapple/coconut
Cakes, sweet potato pies to name a few...
Anything that Grandma cooked
Was delicious as everyone knew...

I must mention the stewed crabs
With dumplings, potatoes and gravy in the pot...
The cake cornbread and the biscuits
Straight out the oven while they're hot...

You are cherished and forever will be
The inspiration till my journey ends...
Keep watching over our family
And greet us when we meet again...

Upon Death

IF I SHOULD DIE TODAY

TRY NOT TO CRY TOO MUCH

EVENTHOUGH IF YOU CARED

IT WOULD BE HARD NOT TO SHED A TEAR...

IF I SHOULD DIE TODAY

BE ENCOURAGED TO KNOW THAT I KNOW GOD

THAT I ACCEPTED HIM AS MY SAVIOUR

AND ABOVE OTHERS, WE WERE AT PEACE...

IF I SHOULD DIE TODAY

KNOW THAT POETRY WAS AT THE
TOP OF MY INSPIRATION

I COULD FEEL PAIN AND NOT PARTAKE OF IT

I FELT JOY IN THE MIDST OF SORROW...

IF I SHOULD DIE TODAY

BELIEVE THAT MY DISPOSITION WAS GUIDED

THAT MY EVERY MOVE WAS
CONCENTRATED BY PRAYER

I WAITED FOR HIS APPROVAL...

IF I SHOULD DIE TODAY

THE REST SHOULD KEEP ON LIVING
LEARN OF GOD'S WORD AND POWER
SHARE, GIVE, TAKE OR REJECT
WHICHEVER IS APPROPRIATE
KNOW THE PARTIALITIES OF LIFE...
IF I SHOULD DIE TODAY
I'D FEEL AS THOUGH I'VE WASTED GOD'S TIME
AS THOUGH THERE WERE YEARS ON
CALENDARS NOT CALCULATED BY ME
KNOW THAT HIS TIME IS NOT OF OURS
BUT OURS MUST BE DEDICATED TO HIM...

Clubfoot Creek